Flashes & Specks

poems by

Diane R. Wiener

Finishing Line Press
Georgetown, Kentucky

Flashes & Specks

Copyright © 2021 by Diane R. Wiener
ISBN 978-1-64662-516-1 First Edition
All rights reserved under International and Pan-American Copyright Conventions.
No part of this book may be reproduced in any manner whatsoever without written permission from the publisher, except in the case of brief quotations embodied in critical articles and reviews.

ACKNOWLEDGMENTS

"Ithaca on Labor Day" and "this Tuesday" were published in the anthology, *Welcome to the Resistance: Poetry as Protest*
"For J., 2.16.18" was published in *Tammy*
"Paradise was consumed" was published in *The South Carolina Review*
"Do the dead read" and "Gassho, Walt" were published in *Queerly*
"Ode to a Siphonophore," "Mid-Sentence, 1918," "Ashes," "Nektonic Larghetto," and "Reputation" appeared originally on Diane R. Wiener's personal website, aka WienerBlog (dianerwiener.com)
The Golem referenced in "this Tuesday" is the same mystical companion featured in *The Golem Verses*, poems by Diane R. Wiener (Nine Mile, 2018)

Publisher: Leah Huete de Maines
Editor: Christen Kincaid
Cover Art: Lucy Loo Wales, "The Origins," https://lucyloowalesdesign.marketing
Author Photo: Diane R. Wiener
Cover Design: Elizabeth Maines McCleavy

Order online: www.finishinglinepress.com
also available on amazon.com

Author inquiries and mail orders:
Finishing Line Press
PO Box 1626
Georgetown, Kentucky 40324
USA

Table of Contents

This morning 1

Blizzard 2

The Medium One 3

For J., 2.16.18 5

Do the dead read 6

Ashes 7

Ithaca on Labor Day 8

Mabon Succoth 9

this Tuesday 10

Paradise was consumed 11

Tagma 12

Ode to a Siphonophore 13

Nektonic Larghetto 15

cuttlefish flashpoints 16

No Fishing Allowed 17

Solstice 18

A Year 19

unleavened 20

Clarinet 21

what if the day 22

Job 23

On Día de los Muertos 24

Mid-Sentence, 1918 25

Gassho, Walt 26

Reputation 27

Flashes and Specks 28

*The doubts of day-time and the doubts of night-time—
the curious whether and how,*

*Whether that which appears so is so, or is it all flashes
and specks?*
　　　　　　—Walt Whitman

*For my friends, family,
and all of the ophthalmologists in my life—
past and present.*

This morning

I turned
into gravity.
Mouth fell
awe breathed.
Inner filaments
magnet careened.
Taffy mind
escaped.
Skin watch
tasted worries
emptied.
Medulla Medea
spiralled
envy ended.
Takeover
turned
evergreen
swept
deimatic.

Blizzard

Sloth icicles
edge my home.
I knocked part of one down.
Its foot-long spine I cradled
then threw into three feet of snow.
A budding paleontologist
on the prowl after what
I already knew was the real deal.

Edited photograph.
Vertebrae intact.

The Medium One

Trees found their way
under the driveway,
likely from next door.

Thirsty, they sought out water.
Some may even be coming
from street-side.

The poet snaked for 70 feet.

Roots clogged the drain.

I could redirect the entire
sewer line to the street
or just have snakes
every few years,

now that trees know where to look,
he said. Then, he
updated the fitting with a fernco
to make it more accessible, in the future.

We agreed that he would cap off
the pipe in the driveway,
redirect the gutter from
the back covered porch, so
it no longer goes into the ground pipe, but,

instead, drains directly to the driveway
via a new, angled tray.

Now, a Gemini gutter downspout
splits the long-term risk
of rain accumulation
backing into a basement.

He taught me that tree roots
form a curtain in sewer lines,
tangle over time into sieves, until eventually
no water passes.

I asked the poet the name
of his not-biggest snake
down my narrow stairs.

The Medium One, he said.

For J., 2.16.18

The night I learned you died,
you taught me carousel horses are friends with birds.
It's not protection, just theirs.
I didn't know.
I hear but cannot see them.
I circle seek.
None appear in perimeter,
but they are surely there.
I look up, cast no spell,
just move within what you called
cyclical nonlinear mythical time.
Then, she appears exactly,
paused in profile, eye level,
as I must descend the stairs,
because the escalator will only rise.
I stop in hope on a step,
she hops, flutters,
mall railings framing her delicate fierceness,
all Rothko angles.
Over a thousand people,
most less than a quarter of your age, each,
and no one knows I weep.
Better that way.
But, I feel the bird knew, as she flew,
facing away from me.
It's always a bird,
isn't it, darling,
it always is.

Do the dead read

Uncaria tomentosa
greetings breathless
in orange smiles

Do the dead read
low rise tide cakes
lined with
woven birds

Do the dead read
adumbrated
barley hemlock

Do the dead read
shapeless combs
dissolved synesthesia
feel mouthless
honeyed marathons
jocund sprints
having nowhere to go
all the time in the world

Ashes

at the base of a
snow-gum eucalyptus

ceasefire turquoise
grasshopper ghosts
swim-dream baby lakes

dead mother pouches
emptied of roos are
eyed by velvet worms

trapdoor spiderlings hatch

a beetle abdomen heat
signals koala mittens

Ithaca on Labor Day

I don't know why
the bugs won't stop
why that car was crushed
but not this one
why the sea star teemed
why the angle of light
why the refutation
why the new old dead beat
why the solace
why the inconsolable
why the trees are stolen
when no one owns them
in the first place
why the first place is
no progenitor
is a lawless
fissured
ecclesiastes

Mabon Succoth

Birds in purple wrappers,
typewriters with feathers,
two sentences, but one.

Pears west toss,
spell cornucopia.

Tapestries air fish
macerate lore,
stop saying lady,
knowing tramp.

Call up the bark,
salt and vine,
mold and gnat.

Chair mountain shores
drink down
strings, hickory.

this Tuesday

count ballots because bullets
don't belong on the bimah

no more arrows in
the Beit Hamikdash no more
vessel veins

lilac a pogrom attic and you
can't blame the cloven for
not waking a Golem who you
think dusts the ramps knowing
stairs are passé

no confederate flag will light
this windfall waking

ignoring your fake names
sanctuary prevails

Paradise was consumed

one night in early November

The feast lasted several hours

No one made that up

You can't foment metaphors
as good as the unchartered

Birch before oak
sleuth bewitched
shoreline glazed

Spate of ash can minutiae
colonic ferryman throat
left eye metal switchback
a machete confession

Tagma

Hylozoist abstract,
Uncertain if daddy
long-legs dragging a door
jam caboose is grieving
yet joyous, nervous and
hopeful, or nothing.
Knitting needles limp
focus, stray from cat water,
take off glasses, scent
the essential squint blow.
Bleak creamsicle hinges,
feet names primitive can
spend an allegory far more
than ours.

Ode to a Siphonophore

you camera snatch
krill and mysids
stem zones
mirror colonies
bases loaded your
medusae locomotive

you know
snow on thorns
may memoir
an undead battery
dancing

you drift
daffodils near
prayer flags
across blinds

you taste
coffee grinds
on the sea floor

you might
miss a spot

pelagic not pandemic

you squint
sheets of eels

you gleam
beside shoal
facing flesh

you whisk
threads brine
lift bucket needles
westward ho

you lean in my
dream a cat
breathing sleeve
cuffs worn white
push delight

you stripe blue
that part thinking
shifts that one
this bit creating
more of your
jelly reed thin

Nektonic Larghetto

yellow brings
cyanotype its insomnia
an arrogant distress as
Berry warned where the
meditating slugs
levitate to meet snail
grasses a rolling donkey
sings you're alive
I left and didn't know
until today but even though
it's not true millipedes
wave nebulae paws
everywhere

cuttlefish flashpoints

quincunx
she named a relation
of no relation
said at this age the game
would be topped
unstoppable
I was pissed then
but she was right

No Fishing Allowed

slivers are convinced
they are better
than nothing

unpolluted coral
shelves tumbling
in the solo bed

shutters stuck open
trapped in empathy

Solstice

as far as I know

this warmest, longest night
makes no distinction between

crunched leaves frozen
skies driven empty
claw cloudy yellow ribbons
lingering in the mindshaft bliss

as far as
not distance learned

across melter floors
fissured optics
arpeggio

A Year

Blue spruce sings
to her dead sister.
Sickly cherry carbon talks
to maple stump.
Pear and I have a rapport, but,
he cannot be my intercessor.
Devotion is not expected.
Too many bricks, no chairs.
Airless room, desiccated petal.
Trees are dogs, judgeless.

unleavened

charoset isn't mortar
red handled chopper
unglued leavetaking
where that wooden
bowl wound up
walnuts apples wine
no one left to ask
shows up often
in the lines

flash heats break
the middle matzoh
unaccounted
bitters believe I was
before eggless copper
salted the walls
in solo liturgy

Clarinet

I'll never know whether you
breathed all the way down

maybe you passed out and
the sea ate your windpipe

a tie flying sideways
didn't hang

I like believing
Paul Robeson hummed
along your 19 stories

scream fused,
dog long gone

I get it, older now
mystery debates

39 isn't 40
a negligible difference

what if the day

didn't begin
film dipped
fire eyed

any reasonable person
wouldn't make me
knowing the lens
will be measured
before the start

expert pizza slicing
routine you opine
to restrained algae
blue-green

I'm just crayons
lit up anesthesia
heels worn down
the usual ways

now it's more like
shatter and suck

sheep feed solar panels
cannot keep cells
hazard guesses
forget the last line

the horses know
it was a good one

Job

A Jacobean elixir
unclenches these
morning fists.
Twilight at periwinkle
phase snaps the
cervical key. Emergency
calls don't go through most
of the time when I try. Can't
stop the archive flood or
find the missing score.
Yellow pages burn last,
whichever stone turns.
He wanted to write
when reeds could have
been enough. Building
chemistry, I wish for wood.

On Día de los Muertos

floating dragons
played astronomy

synechiae cats
taught bone language

fearless
narrow bridges sang

Mid-Sentence, 1918

When I worried, they cut out the elbow rock,
a calcified cyst, no foreign body.
When the blue sheet had worn so much,
it tore into a half square at rest.
When he stared at nothing, I saw a little flotilla.
When war was blurry, the glass chamsa swung.
When edam was all that was left, muenster glided in, surprised.
When the triangle flap was not a sheet,
a malleable unicorn fell in the tear.
When censorship and peace conflated, the just became confused.
When wing fur was the last safe place.

Gassho, Walt
(dandelion snow)

no use crying on
blue goat Shabbat
pigeons could
be doves
onion edge
leaf tilt
red sprout
conifer scar
garlic escape
lupin star

Reputation

Common Grackle you
visit on Boxing Day
through copper
framed Sycamore hanging
underneath two red-crowned
cranes and three crows

not yet a murder
rumor has you at the scene
taking out the smaller
birds your sunspot eye
piercing the Solstice

You're no bully
not an angry jester
a thief or a liar

Sibley says you prefer junipers
are heavier than a blackbird
calls your voice unmusical

I like your keel tail
iridescent privacy
gregarious song
without accusation

Flashes and Specks

right after the fire
a rabbit calmly watched

asphalt at its
marathon midpoint

unrestricted affirmations
ended reptilian smoke

a cormorant called yes

Diane R. Wiener is the author of the poetry collection, *The Golem Verses* (Nine Mile Press, 2018). Diane's poems also appear in *Nine Mile Literary Magazine, Wordgathering, Tammy, Queerly, The South Carolina Review, Welcome to the Resistance: Poetry as Protest, Diagrams Sketched on the Wind, Jason's Connection,* and elsewhere. Her creative nonfiction appears in *Stone Canoe, Mollyhouse,* and *The Abstract Elephant Magazine*; flash fiction appears in volumes 2 and 3 of *Ordinary Madness*. After serving as Guest Editor for *Nine Mile Literary Magazine*'s Special Double Issue on Neurodivergent, Disability, Deaf, Mad, and Crip poetics (Fall 2019), Diane was appointed Assistant Editor. She is the Editor-in-Chief of *Wordgathering: A Journal of Disability Poetry and Literature,* housed at Syracuse University. Diane has published widely on Disability studies and cultures, Mad pride, pedagogy, social justice, and empowerment, among other subjects. She blogged for the *Huffington Post* between May 2016 and January 2018. You can visit Diane online at: https://dianerwiener.com/.

www.ingramcontent.com/pod-product-compliance
Lightning Source LLC
LaVergne TN
LVHW041511070426
835507LV00012B/1496